Written by **Heather E. Schwartz** and **Tammi Salzano**
Designed by **Flora Chan**

an imprint of
■SCHOLASTIC
www.scholastic.com

Scholastic and Tangerine Press and associated logos are trademarks
and/or registered trademarks of Scholastic Inc.

Published by Tangerine Press, an imprint of Scholastic Inc.,
557 Broadway; New York, NY 10012

10 9 8 7 6 5 4 3 2 1

ISBN-10: 0-545-17229-2
ISBN-13: 978-0-545-17229-5

Printed in the U.S.A.

TAKE A TRIP
AROUND THE WORLD

15
BIG B[
London,
England

16

15
14

1
**STATUE OF
LIBERTY**
New York,
United States

2

4

3

14
STONEHENGE
Salisbury Plain,
England

PACIFIC

5

6

OCEAN

ATLANIC

OCEAN

2
**MOUNT
RUSHMORE**
South Dakota,
United States

3
**GRAND
CANYON**
Arizona,
United States

8

9

13
ACROPOLIS
Athens, Greece

4
**NIAGARA
FALLS**
Border of United
States & Canada

5
CHICHÉN ITZÁ
Mexico

7
EASTER ISLAND
Easter Island, Chile;
South Pacific Ocean

7

11
**LEANING
TOWER OF
PISA**
Pisa, Italy

12
**EIFFEL
TOWER**
Paris, France

6
**TEMPLE OF
THE GIANT
JAGUAR**
Guatemala,
Central America

8
**MACHU
PICCHU**
Peru,
South America

9
**AMAZON
RAIN FOREST**
Brazil,
South America

10
**NEUSCHWANSTEIN
CASTLE**
The Bavarian Alps
of Germany

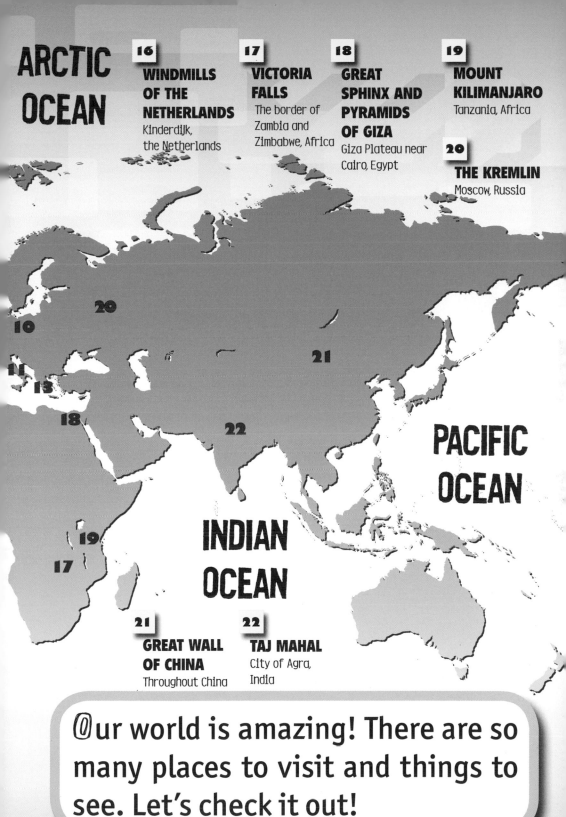

ARCTIC OCEAN

16 WINDMILLS OF THE NETHERLANDS
Kinderdijk, the Netherlands

17 VICTORIA FALLS
The border of Zambia and Zimbabwe, Africa

18 GREAT SPHINX AND PYRAMIDS OF GIZA
Giza Plateau near Cairo, Egypt

19 MOUNT KILIMANJARO
Tanzania, Africa

20 THE KREMLIN
Moscow, Russia

PACIFIC OCEAN

INDIAN OCEAN

21 GREAT WALL OF CHINA
Throughout China

22 TAJ MAHAL
City of Agra, India

Our world is amazing! There are so many places to visit and things to see. Let's check it out!

STATUE OF LIBERTY

The Statue of Liberty was built in 1886. France gave her to the United States as a sign of friendship. The Statue was used as a lighthouse until 1902.

When the wind blows at 50 miles per hour (80 kilometers per hour), the Statue sways 3 inches (7.6 centimeters)!

WHERE IN THE WORLD?
New York Harbor, New York; United States
HOW BIG? 151 feet (46 meters) tall

MOUNT RUSHMORE

Mount Rushmore is a large rock carving. It honors four American presidents: George Washington, Thomas Jefferson, Theodore Roosevelt, and Abraham Lincoln.

Each president's head is as tall as a six story building.

WHERE IN THE WORLD?
The Black Hills of South Dakota; United States

HOW BIG? More than 5,500 feet (1,676 meters) tall

GRAND CANYON

The Grand Canyon is a deep, steep-walled rock formation. It was formed by water erosion (wearing away of the rock) from the Colorado River.

The entire Grand Canyon is tilted. The northern rim is more than 1,000 ft. (305 m) higher than the south rim.

WHERE IN THE WORLD?
Arizona, United States
HOW BIG? 277 miles (446 kilometers) long; 18 miles (29 kilometers) wide; more than 5,000 feet (1,500 meters) deep.

NIAGARA FALLS

The Niagara Falls slam into the ground with tons of force. Amazingly, in 1901, a woman survived a trip over the Falls in a barrel!

Water pours over the Falls at a rate of 757,500 gallons (2,867,449 liters) every second. That's like filling more than 15,000 bathtubs every second!

WHERE IN THE WORLD?
Border of United States and Canada
HOW BIG? Horseshoe (Canadian) Falls: 2,200 feet (670 m) long, 187 feet (57 m) tall
American Falls: 1,075 feet (328 m) long, 182 feet (55 m) tall

Mayans built the city of Chichén Itzá about a thousand years ago. The ruins, including a famous pyramid temple called *Kukulcan*, still stand today.

To get to the top of Chichén Itzá, you have to climb about 91 steps.

WHERE IN THE WORLD? Mexico
HOW BIG? Kukulcan: 75 feet (23 meters) tall

TEMPLE OF THE GIANT JAGUAR

The ancient Mayans built the Temple of the Giant Jaguar more than a thousand years ago. When sunlight hits the roof of the temple, an outline of Ah Cacaw (the ancient leader buried in the temple) can be seen sitting on his throne.

Ancient people who lived on Easter Island carved huge statues called *moai* from volcanic ash. Scientists think that they are symbols of the most powerful chiefs who ruled the island.

➡ There are 887 moai on Easter Island.

WHERE IN THE WORLD?
Easter Island, Chile; South Pacific Ocean
HOW BIG? Tallest moai: 33 feet (10 meters); each moai averages 14 tons (12 T) in weight

MACHU PICCHU

The ancient Incan city of Machu Picchu was lost to the modern world for nearly 400 years. Gold jewelry, human bones, mummies, and musical instruments from the city have been found.

American explorer Hiram Bingham discovered Machu Picchu in 1911.

WHERE IN THE WORLD?
Peru, South America
HOW BIG? About 5 square miles
(13 square kilometers)

AMAZON
RAIN FOREST

The world's largest tropical rain forest is known as the Amazon Rain Forest, or Amazonia. Animals living there include 500 different mammals and 175 kinds of lizards.

→ The Amazon Rain Forest receives more than 100 inches (254 centimeters) of rain every year. That's like stacking $8\frac{1}{2}$ rulers on top of each other.

WHERE IN THE WORLD?
Brazil, South America
HOW BIG? 2,500,011 miles (6,475,000 kilometers)—it covers more than half of Brazil!

NEUSCHWANSTEIN CASTLE

Neuschwanstein Castle was built during the late 1800s. Later, it was the model for Sleeping Beauty's castle at Disneyland!

It took 14 carpenters four years to carve woodwork in the bedroom, but King Ludwig II only slept there eleven nights.

WHERE IN THE WORLD?
The Bavarian Alps of Germany
HOW BIG? About 19,466 square feet (1,808 square meters)

LEANING TOWER
OF PISA

Italy's Leaning Tower of Pisa was built during the Middle Ages as a bell tower with seven bells. They don't ring, however, because the vibrations could cause the structure to collapse.

The tower leans about $\frac{1}{20}$ of an inch (1.27 millimeters) every year, but engineers believe it will last another 200 years.

WHERE IN THE WORLD? Pisa, Italy
HOW BIG? 180 feet (55 meters) tall; 52 feet (16 meters) in diameter at the base

EIFFEL TOWER

The Eiffel Tower was built by Gustav Eiffel for the 1889 World's Fair in Paris, France. Today, most people recognize it as a symbol of France.

Every seven years, workers use 50 tons (45.4 T) of dark brown paint to paint the tower.

WHERE IN THE WORLD?
Paris, France
HOW BIG? 986 feet (301 meters), not including the antenna

ACROPOLIS

The word *Acropolis* comes from the Greek words for "highest city." The monuments of the Acropolis were built on a high, rocky hill so the people would be safe from an invasion.

→ The Parthenon, a temple built to honor the goddess Athena, is the most famous building in the ruins.

WHERE IN THE WORLD?
Athens, Greece

HOW BIG? Built on a limestone hill that rises 500 feet (150 meters) above sea level

STONEHENGE

Stonehenge is made up of huge rectangular stones that stand on end and form a circle. Most scholars believe that Stonehenge was a sacred place of religious rituals or ceremonies.

Construction on Stonehenge is believed to have begun about 5,000 years ago.

WHERE IN THE WORLD?
Salisbury Plain, England
HOW BIG? Largest stones: 49 tons (44.6 T) in weight

BIG BEN

Many people think the famous clock in London is called Big Ben. But that's actually the name for the great bell in the clock tower!

The hour hands on the clock tower are 14 feet (4.3 meters) long. The minute hands measure 9 feet (2.7 meters) in length.

WHERE IN THE WORLD? London, England
HOW BIG? 13 $\frac{1}{2}$ tons (12.2 T)

WINDMILLS OF THE NETHERLANDS

The Kinderdijk-Elshout Mill Network is a collection of windmills. They were built to pump water during floods. Today, they are protected as national monuments.

The 19 windmills were built between 1722 and 1761.

WHERE IN THE WORLD?
Kinderdijk, the Netherlands
HOW BIG? Span of sails: Up to 92 feet (28 meters)

VICTORIA FALLS

Victoria Falls is part of the Zambezi River. Spray from the falls can be spotted from miles away!

→ Locals call Victoria Falls *Mosi-oa-Tunya*, which means "the smoke that thunders."

WHERE IN THE WORLD?
The border of Zambia and Zimbabwe, Africa
HOW BIG? 5,604 feet (1,708 meters) wide; 328 feet (100 meters) tall

GREAT SPHINX & PYRAMIDS OF GIZA

The Great Sphinx is a huge stone statue with the head of a human and the body of a lion. It's believed to guard the Great Pyramids of Giza.

The Great Sphinx was carved from a single piece of limestone that was used to build the pyramids.

WHERE IN THE WORLD?
Giza Plateau near Cairo, Egypt
HOW BIG? Sphinx: 66 feet (20 meters) tall, 240 feet (73 meters) long; Great Pyramids: Range from 218 feet (66 meters) to 449 feet (137 meters) tall

MOUNT KILIMANJARO

Mount Kilimanjaro, the tallest mountain in Africa, is actually a volcano! It has three volcanic cones, called Kibo, Mawenzi, and Shira.

A local guide named Simon Mtuy holds the record for the fastest round-trip climb. He made it to the top and back down again in 8 hours and 27 minutes.

WHERE IN THE WORLD? Tanzania, Africa
HOW BIG? 19,340 feet (5,895 meters) tall

THE KREMLIN

A palace, a bell tower, and gold-topped cathedrals are among the beautiful buildings that make up the Kremlin. It is now the seat of government for Russia.

The word *Kremlin* means "walled city."

WHERE IN THE WORLD?
Moscow, Russia
HOW BIG? 90 acres
(36 hectares)

GREAT WALL OF CHINA

Construction of the Great Wall of China began thousands of years ago. Rulers used it as protection against attacks.

→ The Great Wall of China is made of wood boards, bricks, rocks, and planks. It took thousands of years to link all the sections together.

WHERE IN THE WORLD? Throughout China
HOW BIG? Average height: 23–26 feet (7–8 meters) tall; average length: 4,500 miles (7,242 kilometers) long

TAJ MAHAL

The Taj Mahal is one of the Seven Wonders of the World. It took 22 years and more than 20,000 workers to complete the building in 1653.

More than 1,000 elephants were used to move the building materials.

WHERE IN THE WORLD?
City of Agra, India

HOW BIG? The height of the dome is about 114 feet (35 meters); square platform is about 186 square feet (56 square meters); each tower is about 133 feet (40.5 meters) in height.

CONCLUSION

Now, you have been around the world. Ask your parents to help you look on the internet for other places to visit. There are so many places to visit. Our world is amazing!

1

MOUNT FUJI
Honshu Island, Japan

2

GREAT BARRIER REEF
Northeast Coast of Australia

3

TOWER OF LONDON
London, England

4

AYERS ROCK (ULURU)
Northern Territory, Central Australia